Let's Make Something Fun!

by Emilie Barnes

Illustrations by Michal Sparks

HARVEST HOUSE PUBLISHERS

Eugene, Oregon

Let's Make Something Fun!

Text Copyright © 2001 by Emilie Barnes
Published by Harvest House Publishers
Eugene, OR 97402

Library of Congress Cataloging-in-Publication Data

Barnes, Emilie.
    Let's make something fun! / by Emilie Barnes ; illustrations by Michal Sparks.
      p. cm.
    ISBN 0-7369-0530-8
    1. Handicraft for girls—Juvenile literature. [1. Handicraft.] I. Sparks, Michal, ill. II. Title.

TT171 B345 2001
745.5-dc21   00-066980

Some material in this book has previously appeared in:
My Best Friend and Me by Emilie Barnes with Anne Christian Buchanan (Harvest House Publishers, 1997)
Making My Room Special by Emilie Barnes with Anne Christian Buchanan (Harvest House Publishers, 1999)
The Very Best Christmas Ever by Emilie Barnes with Anne and Elizabeth Buchanan (Harvest House Publishers, 1998)

Design and Production: Garborg Design Works, Minneapolis, Minnesota

Printed in Hong Kong

01 02 03 04 05 06 07 08 09 10 / NG /   10 9 8 7 6 5 4 3 2 1

Contents

Making Up Fun on a Rainy Day

Hi, I'm Emilie Marie, and I'm glad you could come over on

this wet and windy day. Christine, Aleesha, and Maria are already here. We're expecting Elizabeth and Jasmine, the other two Angels—that's the name of our friendship club— any minute now.

Earlier this morning, none of us thought that today would turn out to be any fun. We were all ready to go swimming at this great outdoor pool with water-slides, and then it started to

rain—in the middle of the summer! Just as I was groaning about spending a boring day inside watching the rain fall, my mom walked into my room with a big decorated storage box. I'd almost forgotten—my craft box!

So I got on the phone and called up Christine. She remembered a craft she'd learned at school that she's wanted to show me. Then, when I was still on the phone with her, Jasmine came on Christine's call waiting (you know, when you hear that "beep" and someone else is on the other line). She had just gotten back from visiting her cousin Hannah, and she had even more ideas about neat stuff to make. And *then* Aleesha came on *my* call waiting. She's the one who had planned the swimming outing in the first place, so she was really sad about the rain. But she and her little sister, Marti, just got back from summer camp, where they took Arts and Crafts classes and made tons of cool things.

Suddenly all this rain was looking pretty good!

"Okay," I told Christine, "I'll call back Aleesha and I'll also call Elizabeth. You can call Jasmine and Maria and let them know it's an official Angels Craft Day!"

So that's how it happened.  And now here we all are, setting things up at the big worktable in my family room. We're listening to some of our favorite CDs—Christine brought her reggae CD, Aleesha brought piano music, and Maria brought some movie soundtracks. My mom just came in with a big plate of brownies and some toasty-warm cups of raspberry tea. (The Angels love tea parties!) Our craft boxes are ready to go, and so are we.

Let's get started and make something fun!

1 Before You Begin Crafting

When we first started making crafts, we Angels learned the hard way that a little bit of planning guarantees a lot of fun—and some finished crafts! On our first Craft Day when we made Mother's Day cards, we ran out of glue, the black marker ran out of ink, and we ran out of time. Here are seven easy steps we learned that have made the rest of our Craft Days go a whole lot better.

1. Read the directions—all the way through. This is really important! Reading through what you need to do lets you know what steps are coming up and what you'll need to be prepared for. (If I remember, it really helps me to read through twice!) By reading the directions, you'll know what materials you need to have on hand—and what you might need to buy or borrow before you start the craft—and you'll be ready for any steps you might not have done before. If there's something you don't understand, ask an adult or a friend for help before you begin. You can also practice some steps on a piece of scrap material before you do them on your real project.

2. Have an adult standing by. That means your mom or dad or grandmother—whoever is in the house with you and can give you some help. For instance, Christine's mom likes to work on her scrapbooking when we do crafts at her house. When we need help using a sharp craft knife or a hot glue gun or when we just don't understand something, we go into the room where her mom is working, and she's always happy to help us. (We're also learning a lot about making scrapbooks!)

3. Get your work area ready. Before you start gluing, cutting, and getting out the tiny beads and glitter, choose a good work area. At my house we use a big table in the family room. We spread an old sheet on top to protect the table surface. At Maria's house we lay a bunch of newspapers on the floor and just sit down and work there. Christine has a dog and Jasmine has a baby brother, so we never work on the floor at their houses. We keep everything up out of reach and make sure the floor stays clear of any craft materials.

4. Gather all your materials together before you start. We've listed what you need at

the beginning of each craft, so that makes it easy. All of the Angels have our own craft boxes, and we keep all sorts of things in them that might come in handy for a project—scraps of material, colored pens, pieces of yarn, pretty beads. If your list of materials calls for something you don't have, see if one of your friends has the item. Or make a list of what you need for this craft and

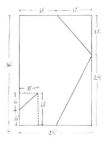

future crafts, then take a trip to your local craft store. It's always a fun place to go, and sometimes they even offer craft classes!

5. When everything's ready, follow the directions step by step.

Sometimes you just want to move on to the fun stuff—the painting or the glitter or the drawing—but it's important that you complete each step so that your craft will turn out like you hope it will.

6. Clean up as you go—and clean up completely when you're finished. When you're finished with one step, take a little bit of time to put the lids on your   markers, put the beads back in their container, or throw away scraps of paper or fabric. That way, cleanup won't take so long. It's also important to clean up as you go when you're at a friend's house. You don't want to leave your friend with a big mess—

just when you have to go home. It's better to clean up together.

7. Enjoy the process! Sometimes when I'm making crafts, I'm so into how the finished product will look that I forget to have fun in the making. So have fun doing the gluing, stringing, and cutting. Slow down if you need to concentrate on a step and take a break to eat something and talk with your friend or your mom. You'll not only have a terrific-looking craft at the end— you'll also have great memories of a really fun day!

Super Things to Make in the Spring

2 There are so many things I love about spring—the first daffodils and tulips that come up in our flower garden, putting on my raincoat and boots and splashing around in puddles, celebrating Easter by going to a sunrise service with my family and having an Easter brunch and egg hunt at my Aunt Evelyn's house. I always get so many ideas for things that I want to make in the spring. The Angels like to spend rainy spring mornings inside working on crafts, then head outside to play when the sun comes out. If it's still rainy when we're finished, we just grab our raingear and go out anyway!

Designer Paper Dolls

My special friend Christine and I have known each other practically since we were babies.

And we've been playing with dolls almost as long! Christine loves to choose clothes for her dolls, and she's learning to sew some of her own outfits. She'll probably be a fashion designer when she grows up! We made these paper dolls one stormy spring day when we were sketching outfit ideas and I said, "Wouldn't it be neat to put

these on your doll?" After you make this Emilie Marie paper doll and these outfits, you can create some outfits of your own!

You will need:
- *scissors*
- *glue*
- *heavy paper (cardboard, cardstock, or a large index card)*

1. Cut around the paper doll on the dotted line.

2. Glue the paper doll onto heavier paper. (A large index card works great!)

3. After the glue has dried, carefully cut the solid black line around Emilie Marie and her base.

4. To make her stand up, slide the slot of the base into the slot of the Emilie Marie doll.

5. Carefully cut out Emilie Marie's outfits. Be sure not to cut the tabs off!

Ponytail Pals

Maria, Elizabeth, and Aleesha all play on the same soccer team. The coach of their team, Coach Kelly, makes them work hard, but she's also a lot of fun. The team made these ponytail pals before a big tournament this spring. Then they decorated them in their team colors. All of the girls—and Coach Kelly—brought them for the games—and they won the tournament! If you use an old sock that's lost its mate, making this doll will cost you almost nothing. (Unless you are used to cutting and sewing fabric, ask an adult to help you with the scissors and the needle. Coach Kelly helped the girls with this step.)

You will need:
- *1 crew sock—the kind with a smooth "foot" and ribbed top. You can make your doll any size you want, but a larger adult sock might be easiest to work with.*
- *1/2 cup rice*
- *polyester fiberfill*
- *2 rubber bands or elastic ponytail holders*
- *short pencil or stick to support neck*
- *scissors sharp enough to cut cloth*
- *tacky craft glue or fabric glue*
- *needle and thread*

To decorate your doll:
markers, fabric paint, felt or fabric scraps, beads, buttons, charms, ribbon, lace scraps, fabric glue

1

1. Begin by pouring the rice into the toe of the sock. This will weight your doll and help it stand upright.

rice

2. Stuff in fiberfill until the sock is stuffed up to the point where

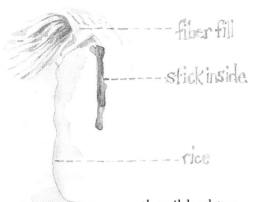

fiber fill

stick inside

rice

the ribbed top begins. Don't stuff the sock too tightly. Poke a short piece of pencil or stick down into the middle of the fiberfill so that its top comes a little below the ribbed top.

3. Wrap one rubber band around the base of the ribbed part to make the ponytail. Wrap another rubber band, more loosely, right below the heel of the sock to make a neck. Adjust stuffing and rubber band to make a nice head shape.

4. Carefully cut the ribbed area into long strips. Try to make the strips the same size and length. Be careful not to cut them off!

5. Now for the fun part! Glue beads on your doll for eyes and mouth. Use markers for hair, eyelashes, and eyebrows. Soft pink cheeks will look so pretty! Tie a bow around her ponytail. String the pearl beads to make a fancy necklace. Glue the buttons on her body. You might add a paper heart with a special message.

Colorful Paper Carnations

One of my favorite spring holidays is Mother's Day. I like to make my mom breakfast in

bed and give her coupons that are good for household chores, things like clearing off the dinner dishes for a week, doing the ironing for a week, or doing something else that isn't one of my regular jobs. The Angels got together the weekend before

Mother's Day to make these pretty flowers for our moms and grandmothers. They were a big hit—and they still look fresh months later!

You will need:
- *2 colors of tissue paper (like red and white) cut into lots of 3" x 3" squares*
- *florist's wire or long green pipe cleaners*
- *green florist's tape*

1. Make a stack of five squares of tissue, alternating the two colors. Fold the stack back and forth like a fan, then pinch the folded stack in the middle and wrap a piece of wire around it, twisting the wire together below the paper to make a stem.

2. With scissors, cut a row of little notches into each end of the folded stack. Then, one by one, pull apart the individual squares of tissue paper to form petals. Fluff out the petals to finish your flower.

3. To decorate my mom's breakfast tray, I made a bunch of these carnations. I also made some plain solid colored ones. She loved them!

3 Sunny Summer Crafts

If you're anything like the Angels, you live for summer! You can play outdoors just about any day, go on fun trips with your family, read books and drink lemonade all day long, or have a blast at summer camp. Crafts are perfect for filling those long, lazy summer days when it seems like all your friends are on vacation and there isn't a lot to do. The Angels also like getting together with whoever's in town to make crafts outside on the patio or under a big shade tree. We always make sure we have some pocket money for ice cream!

Beaded "Hi" Pins

These little beaded pins are fun and easy to make. Jasmine's cousin Hannah taught her how to make them when she visited her this summer. Hannah gives them to new friends when school starts in the fall.

To make one pin, you will need:

- *14 #0 (7/8") safety pins— silver or brass*
- *1 #3 (2") safety pin— silver or brass*
- *clear acrylic spray sealer—if you're using brass safety pins*
- *a package of "seed beads" in assorted colors*
- *1 pair needle-nosed pliers*

(ask your mom or dad if you already have one at your house)
- *a metal fingernail file or a dull letter opener*

1. First, if you are using brass pins, spray them with the sealer to keep them from tarnishing. Ask an adult to help you do this outside. Spread the pins on newspaper, spray, let dry, turn over, then spray again.

2. Spread a bunch of seed beads out on a flat surface and look at them closely. They don't look the same! Some are thick, like little barrels, and some are flatter, like little doughnuts. The doughnut kind works best for this pin.

3. To start the pin, carefully open one of the #0 (smallest) safety pins. You're going to be stringing the beads onto the point of the pin. Now look at the chart on page 21; it shows you how to string the beads. Each square stands for one bead, and each up-and-down column of squares stands for the beads on one safety pin. For instance, column 1 is a stack of black squares. So take that first safety pin and put seven black beads on it. Close the safety pin. (If you have trouble fitting all the beads on the pin or closing it, take all the beads off and look for flatter "doughnuts.")

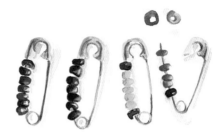

4. With the pliers, carefully pinch the pin as shown to keep it from popping open. Then lay it down on the table and make another just like it— as the second column of the chart shows. Lay it down next to the first pin.

5. Column 3 on the chart is a little different. It shows one black bead, five yellow beads, and another black one. Open a third pin and put black and yellow beads on it to match the chart. (The bottom bead on the chart goes on the pin first.) Close

the pin, pinch with pliers, and put it down. Repeat the process for every row in the chart. Lay the pins down on the table in the order that you finish them: 1, 2, 3, 4, and so on.

6. When you've finished putting beads on all the pins, open the big (#3) safety pin and use the nail file to push open the little loop-the-loop at the end of it. Ask an adult to help you do this. The idea is to push the loop open sideways so you can slide the little safety pins around it. (They get a roller-coaster ride!)

7. Hold the head of the big pin in your left hand with the sharp point facing *away* from you. Pick up the *last* safety pin you beaded (number 14). Hold its head in your right hand with the beads facing away from you and slide the loop at its base onto

the pointed end of the big pin. Push it down and around the loop-the-loop, then push it up the other side of the pin and up against the head. Do the same thing for all your little pins, working from right to left (the last pin you beaded to the first). Make sure

that the beads on all the pins face the same way— and don't stick yourself on the big safety pin!

■ black
☐ yellow
▨ red

8. When you're through putting on the little pins, the beads should spell out "HI." Pin the big pin to your shirt or sweater and wear it, or give it to a friend!

Silver-and-Gold Friendship Bracelets

"Make new friends, but keep the old. One is silver and the other gold." That's an old song that Aleesha and her little sister, Marti, learned at summer camp. They also learned how to make these pretty bracelets during Arts and Crafts time. When Aleesha came home, she couldn't wait to teach us the song—and to show us how to make the bracelets. They're easy to make for your new friends and your old ones—and especially for your forever friends. Look for the beads and the floss in a hobby store or large discount store.

You will need:
- *1 package metallic silver embroidery floss*
- *1 package metallic gold embroidery floss*
- *13 gold 6mm beads*
- *scissors*
- *ruler or yardstick*
- *craft glue*
- *old clipboard or tabletop*
- *tape*

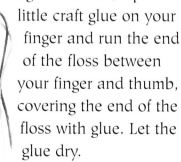

1. Measure and cut one piece of gold floss and one piece of silver—each 48" long—and seal the ends to keep the floss from unraveling. To do this, squeeze a little craft glue on your finger and run the end of the floss between your finger and thumb, covering the end of the floss with glue. Let the glue dry.

2. Hold the two pieces of floss together and fold them in half. You will need to have two strands (one of each color) longer than the other two. Pull one strand of silver and one of gold until they are about 30" long. Then you will have four strands of floss with a loop at one end. Hold the floss at the loop end and carefully tie an overhand knot as shown, leaving a little loop above the knot. The loop should be just big enough for one of the beads to go through.

3. If you have a clipboard, place the knot in the "clip" part of the clipboard so that the loose ends of the thread are facing you. (If you don't have a clipboard, tape the top loop and the center strands to a table.) Arrange the threads as shown in the picture, with the short gold and silver threads together in the center and the other two longer threads on the outside. Tape the center threads down at the bottom of the clipboard. Hold their ends together and coat them with glue. Let the glue dry, then cut across the glued-together strands at an angle. This will make it easier to string the beads.

4. Now you can begin to tie the knots that make the bracelet. You will only be tying knots with the *outside* threads. The ones in the center will stay still, and you'll tie the knots around them. Each knot (a square knot) is made in two steps.

Step 1: Pick up the left-hand thread and cross *it over* the center and *under* the right-hand thread, leaving a loop on the left. Next take the right-hand thread and bring it *over* the left-hand thread, pass it *under* the center threads, and bring it up *through* the loop on the left. Pull gently on both outside threads until they form an even circle or oval around the center threads running in the middle. Then pull the circle into a *firm* knot.

Step 2: This step is just like the previous one, but backward. Pick up the right-hand thread and cross it *over* the center, leaving a loop on the right. Bring the left-hand thread *over* the right-hand thread, *under* the center threads, and up *through* the right-hand loop. Pull the threads even, then tighten. With the two steps together, you've just completed a square knot. (Note: Working with the two colors of thread makes it easy to remember which step you just did. If you begin step 1 with the silver thread on the left, after step 1 it will be on the right. It will move back over to the left after you've finished step 2. So whenever the silver is on the left, you'll know you've finished the entire knot.)

5. Repeat steps 1 and 2 until you've completed about 1/2" of the bracelet. Then you're ready to put on the first bead. First, untape the two center strands. Hold their ends together, take a single gold bead, and thread it onto the double center strand. Slide the bead up against the finished part of the bracelet, then tape down the center strands again.

6. Bring the two outside strands around the outside of the bead and make a square knot (two steps) right below the bead. Continue making square knots for another 1/2", then add another bead, then 1/2" of knotting, another bead, and another 1/2" of knotting.

7. You should now have three beads on your bracelet along with your knotting. To make a flower, slide one bead onto the center strands and three beads onto each of the outside threads. Push all the beads up against your previous work and make another square knot right below the beads, pulling the thread firmly. Adjust the beads if necessary to form the flower shape.

8. Keep on knotting and adding beads until you have three more beads. Finish with 1/2" of knotting.

9. To finish your bracelet, untape the center strands and hold all the strands together. Tie another overhand knot, and push it close up against the bracelet. Then tie another knot right over that one, then make another knot if necessary to make a knot just big enough to go through the loop on the other end of the bracelet. Pull all the strands in the knot really tight, then cut off the ends close to the knot. Add a little dab of craft glue at the place where you cut the ends off, just to make sure they won't unravel. Let the glue dry. Fasten your bracelet by slipping the knotted end through the loop.

10. After you've learned to make this pretty bracelet, you can make it with lots of different kinds of thread and beads. Try thick embroidery thread, natural-colored hemp, waxed-line cord, or even plain old yarn. Almost any kind of bead will work as long as the hole in the middle is big enough to go on the doubled center threads. Try making a whole bracelet out of knots and bead flowers. Or, for an interesting variation, make a bracelet using only step 1 or only step 2. The bracelet will twist around in a spiral!

Keep-in-Touch Cards

This cute pop-up card is a nice way to keep in touch with friends who are on vacation. Elizabeth spent most of the summer at her grandmother's house. She had a lot of fun, but she missed her friends. So the Angels got together and we each made her one of these cards. Then we mailed her one card a week! I made her a happy face card (like

the one on p. 30), Maria made her a red, white, and blue Fourth-of-July card with sparkly glitter that looked just like fireworks, and Aleesha made her a cheerful sunflower card. Once you learn how it works, you can use the same idea to make birthday and other cards, too.

You will need:
- *1 sheet (8 1/2" x 11") construction paper, card stock, or other heavy paper*
- *1 scrap (at least 3" x 6")*

*bright yellow construction
paper, card stock, or other
heavy paper*

- *ruler*
- *pencil*
- *scissors*
- *markers to decorate,
  including thick-line black
  marker*
- *craft glue*

1. Fold the
8 1/2" x 11"
sheet of
construction
paper in half
and then in half
again. Unfold the card and lay it
down on the table in front of you
like an open book, with the
"inside" facing up and one of the
long sides toward you. There
should be two opened-up folds
criss-crossing the paper, dividing
the card into four equal parts.

2. Use your ruler to measure
2 1/4" in from the top right corner. Make a small mark there
with your pencil. Make another
mark 3 1/4" from the corner.
Make two more marks 2 1/4"
and 3 1/4"
from the
bottom
right
corner.

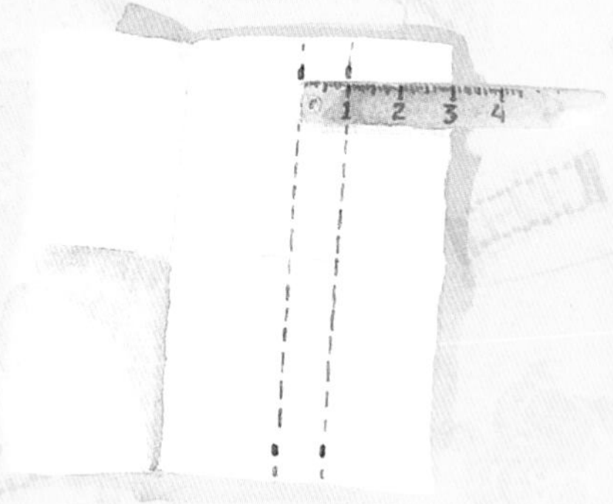

Connect the marks as shown by drawing two very light pencil lines running down the middle of the right-hand side of the card. Notice that the longer opened-out fold cuts the two lines you drew in half. Measure 1" up from this fold on each line and make another very light pencil mark.

3. Fold the card along the long fold you just measured from, with the pencil marks on the outside. Cut along the lines you drew from the fold to the 1" pencil marks. Now fold back the little tab you just cut out as

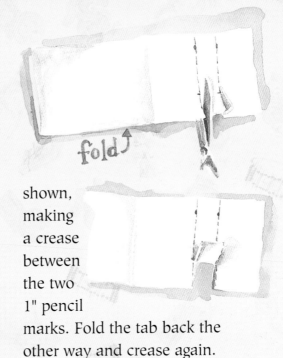

fold

shown, making a crease between the two 1" pencil marks. Fold the tab back the other way and crease again.

4. Unfold the card, then fold again with the short sides together and the pencil lines on the inside. Place the card before you with the fold to your left. Slip your finger under your scissor cuts and pull the cut-out

5. Use the bottom of a jar or bottle to trace two circles (about 2" across) on another piece of paper. Use a black marker to draw happy features on one and sad features on the other. Also, outline the faces with a thick, wavy black line to help them stand out from the card.

piece gently toward you. The cutout will fold in the middle to form a little half-box. This is the "pop up" part of the card. Press the card closed to crease edges of pop-up box. Then open the card and carefully erase all the pencil marks.

6. Hold the cut-out card as shown in the picture and glue the bottom of the happy face to the front of the "box." Let the glue dry. Then close the card and glue the sad face on the front. Use a marker to write the message on the outside ("This is me without you!") and inside of the card ("This is me with you!"). If you want to draw "sunbeams" around your happy face, do it with the card partly open so the beams are around the "popped up" face.

7. You can make all sorts of different cards using this idea. For instance, you can glue a heart instead of a happy face to the pop-up box and ask your friend to "Have a Heart." Or you can use this idea to make a birthday card or a valentine. Use your imagination.

This is me with you! Can we be friends again? Love, Frank.

Fantastic Fall Arts and Crafts

4 If I were to say "Hot spiced cider, warm wool sweaters, and falling leaves," could you guess the season? That's right—fall! The Angels look forward to autumn because even though we love summer, we like all the things that this season brings. We also like to get together on the weekends to make crafts because we don't get to see each other as much as we do during the summer. Some of us go to public schools (but we aren't always in the same class), some of us go to private schools, and some of us are home-schooled. So fall Angel Craft Days are extra special. We like to go to Maria's house because her father is a baker and we always eat freshly baked cinnamon rolls in front of the fireplace before we get going on our crafts!

High-Flying Friendship Kites

September is such a great month. You sometimes have to wear a jacket or sweater outside, but it's usually sunny out. And the afternoons can get really windy—perfect for flying a kite!

Jasmine's dad makes and flies stunt kites, and we all like to watch him fly them down at the park. This isn't a stunt kite, but it is easy to make and fun to fly. You can get together a group of friends and paint each other's faces on your kites. Then take them all to an open field on a windy day and see whose face soars the highest.

To make a friendship kite you will need:
- *a large sheet of wrapping paper or newsprint (36" x 24") for the pattern*
- *1 plastic garbage bag, "kitchen" size or larger (white ones are easier to decorate)*
- *3/16" wooden dowel, 36" long*
- *yardstick and ruler*
- *pencil*
- *black permanent marker (thin point)*
- *scissors*
- *acrylic craft paints and brushes*
- *clear tape*
- *hole punch*
- *strips of fabric for tail*
- *kite string*
- *optional: craft knife and adult help*

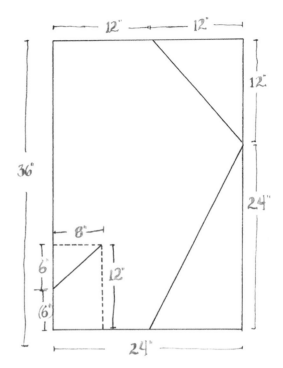

1. To make the pattern, use a yardstick to mark off on the sheet of paper. Cut it out.

2. Spread out the plastic bag on a table. (If needed, cut the top and bottom so the bag lies flat.) You should have a double layer

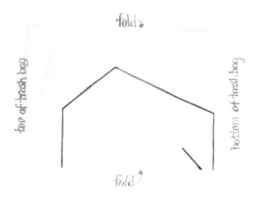

top of trash bag

fold↘

bottom of trash bag

fold↗

of plastic with folds on both sides. Lay the pattern with the long edge against one of the folds and trace around the pattern with the permanent marker. Cut out your half-kite. Cut the triangle-shaped vent as shown in the diagram.

3. Unfold your kite and strengthen all the corners with pieces of transparent tape.

Then decorate your kite any way you want to with acrylic paints. Since you're making kites with your friends, why not paint portraits of each other?

4. Measure 18" down from the end of the dowel and mark it with a pencil line. This is where you want to cut your dowel in half. The easiest way is to hold it down on a table with the pencil mark at the edge, then quickly break off the part that hangs off the table. This leaves sort of a ragged edge, but it won't hurt your kite. If you want a smoother cut, ask an adult to do it with a craft knife.

5. Tape the two dowel halves to the kite as shown. Use a hole punch to make holes in the outside corners. Then tape two or more strips of cloth along the bottom of the kite to make the tails. (Start with two tails about 18" long. You might need to experiment with the length and placement of the tails to help your kite fly better.)

6. Cut a 10-foot piece of kite string to make a bridle. Tie the two ends of the bridle to the two holes in the side of the kite. Then find the center of the bridle and make a knotted loop as shown. Tie the kite string to the loop. Then take your kite to an open place and run to help it get in the air.

What's Happening Bulletin Boards

Fall is an exciting season because so much is going on—school, sporting events, music lessons (I'm learning to play the violin), and other fun activities. But sometimes it's really hard to keep track of

bridle

tie string on here

everything. I've found that it helps me to have one main place to put important notes and papers—and a big stack on my desk doesn't count. (I can't find anything that way!) This cute bulletin board is perfect for holding schedules, homework reminders, notes from friends, important phone numbers, pictures, and other treasures. It also doesn't require any pushpins; just tuck everything under the ribbons. You can make it in colors to match your room!

You will need:
- *24" by 18" piece of foam-core board from a hobby shop*
- *26" by 20" piece of fabric ironed smooth*
- *tacky craft glue*
- *package of thumbtacks*
- *about 5 feet of 1/2" ribbon in colors to go with your fabric*
- *scissors and a ruler or yardstick*
- *decorations (buttons, bows, more ribbon, lace, silk flowers, paper cutouts)*
- *picture frame to fit foam-core board (if you want)*
- *thick piece of polyester batting (if you want)*

1. Place the fabric wrong side up on a flat surface and lay the foam-core board in the middle. The same amount of

cloth should be sticking out all around.

2. Start gluing on one of the short sides. Put a line of glue along the back of the board near this edge, but stop before you get to the corners. Wrap the extra fabric on that side around to the back and press it into the glue. Push in several thumbtacks to hold down the fabric while the glue dries. Do the same thing with the other short side and both of the long sides. Make sure the fabric is pulled smooth across the front of the foam-core board. Glue the corners last. You'll probably have to fold down or bunch the fabric before you glue it down. If it's really bulky, you can cut away some of the extra before you glue.

3. Let the glue dry, then turn the board over. The pretty, covered side should be facing you. Cut a piece of ribbon long enough to go from one top corner to the opposite bottom corner, plus two inches. Cut another piece of ribbon the same length. Lay these two ribbons from corner to corner in an "X" shape, leaving about an inch of ribbon hanging off each corner. Stick in thumbtacks at the center of the "X" and the four corners to hold the ribbon in place.

4. Use your ruler to measure about six inches from the two corners on the short sides and eight inches from the corners on the long sides. Stick in a thumbtack to mark the spots where you measured. You should have three tacks on each side. Now cut pieces of ribbon long enough to stretch from thumbtack to thumbtack in a criss-cross pattern (see picture), plus an extra two inches for each ribbon. Lay the ribbons across the board as shown, then pull out each "marker" thumbtack and use it to hold the ribbon in place at the edge of the board.

5. Turn over the board. Pull the ends of the ribbon around and

glue to the back of the board— use tacks to hold them down while glue dries. Then, if you want to, remove all "holder" tacks from the back of the board. Turn the board over and remove all tacks from the edges. For every place where the ribbons cross each other, stick in a tack whose point has been dipped in glue.

6. To hang your bulletin board, use two stick-on fabric-type hangers. (You can find them in a hardware store.) Attach them to either a long side or a short side at about the point where the ribbons are glued.

7. Now it's time to decorate your bulletin board! Use craft glue or a hot glue gun (with adult help) to cover the edges and the thumb-tacks with buttons, bows, silk flowers, or paper cutouts. After the glue is dry, your bulletin board is ready to hang and use.

A Friend's Gallery

Every fall, the Angels give each other their new school pictures. I used to keep them in a desk drawer or tuck them away in a photo album, but nobody ever saw them that way. Then I learned how to make these fun frames! This is a great way to display pictures of your friends, your family, and even your pets. You can also frame some of your favorite summer pictures. Aleesha took pictures of us learning to roller-blade during the summer, and she framed a whole bunch of them and displayed them on her bedside table. They look hilarious!

Easy Stand-Up Frame

This cute frame holds a wallet-sized photo (like a friend's school picture) perfectly!

- *newspapers*
- *piece of 8 1/2" x 11" cardstock, construction paper, or thin cardboard (Cardstock is thicker than notebook paper and thinner than posterboard—sort of like an index card. You can get it at an art store or office supply place. Its smooth surface makes a nice frame.)*
- *small piece of posterboard (for the stand)*
- *scissors*
- *craft glue or glue stick*
- *ruler*
- *pencil*
- *picture to frame (I framed a photo that was little bigger than 2" x 3".)*
- *stickers, paint, or other decorations for trim*
- *thin plastic page protector (from an office store) to make the "glass" in the frame (optional)*

1. Protect your work area with newspapers. Then take your cardstock and carefully fold it in half, like a

fold

1

2 **fold →**

greeting card (see diagram 1). Fold in half again, pressing the folds firmly with your fingers (diagram 2). Hold the folded piece so that it opens like a book and the folded edge is at the bottom. Make a light pencil mark in the center to show where your picture will go (diagram 3).

3

fold →

fold

2. Open the cardstock, which is now divided into four sections. Find the section with the mark and make another mark on the *back* of the same section. Use a ruler and a pencil to draw in the opening for the window around this second mark (diagram 4). Have fun with different shapes—a heart, a circle, a tilted square, etc.

4 **cut out**

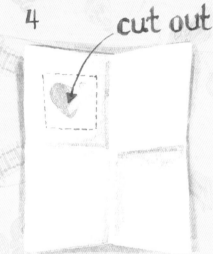

3. To cut out the window, pinch the center of this section with your fingers and snip the pinched part with the scissors. Now you can get your scissors in to cut around the lines.

4. Turn the cardstock over and slip your picture behind the window to see how it fits. Move it around until it looks just right. Then hold the picture in place and turn the frame over. Trace around the outside of the picture. You can also cut out a piece of thin plastic from a page protector to make a "glass" for your frame.

5. Now grab your glue! Make sure the "wrong" side of the cardstock (with the pencil marks) is facing you. First, spread a narrow line of glue around the outside edges of the two sections at the right. Next, carefully spread glue in a "U" shape around the "window" opening. Leave a little space around the picture outline, and don't put any glue above the outline (diagram 5).

5

glue

fold bottom half up

6. Fold the bottom half of the picture up to meet the top half. Press firmly, then fold again along the original second fold. Place under a book until glue is dry. Now you have what looks

6

glue

7

glue on
one side of fold → fold

like a book without pages—with the cut-out window on the "cover." Glue the "book" together (diagram 6).

7. For the stand, use posterboard and cut a small rectangle. Fold diagonally, as shown (diagram 7). Glue onto back of frame.

8. Now move the folded corner to a position where it holds your frame up. Insert the photo (and "glass") into the front through the unglued top edge. Then use paint pens, markers, stickers, and other things to decorate your frame!

Wonderful Winter Creations

5 I love all of the seasons, but winter has to be *my* absolute favorite because that's when *my* absolute favorite holiday—Christmas—is! I'm learning lots of Christmas traditions from my family and from my friends' families too. The Angels always start off the season by making Advent calendars together. We even have our own "Christmas club," where we go to each other's houses to share family traditions. My mother is half-Jewish, so we light a menorah at Hanukkah. And Maria's family is Mexican, so we always head to her house for a special Mexican hot chocolate drink that all of us love. Elizabeth's family has a big New Year's Eve celebration for all of our families. And making crafts to give as holiday gifts is a tradition that's fun for everyone!

The Very Best Christmas Card Ever

We do a lot of Christmas projects with all of the Angels, but as best friends Christine and I have our own special traditions. First we help each other decorate our rooms for Christmas, then we make our own cards. We've made a lot of different kinds of cards, but we call this one the

(go to page 51)

cut here

Front of Card

May You Have the Very Best Christmas Ever!

Made by _____
and Michal Sparks

glue here

glue here

Inside of House

48

Love and joy come to you,
    And to your wassail too!
And God bless you and send you
    A Happy New Year.
And God send you a Happy New Year!

TRADITIONAL ENGLISH CAROL

Dear _____,
I hope your Christmas
is very _____
_____.
You're a special gift to
me because_____
_____.

Love,

_____

Inside of Card

49

very best Christmas card ever. I think you'll like it, too!

You will need:
- *glue or paste*
- *scissors*
- *craft knife*
- *pen*

1. Decorate the front of the house (page 45) with cut-out shapes, wreaths, and bows. Cut it out.

2. Decorate the inside of the house (page 47) by gluing or pasting cut-out shapes in the boxes.

3. Cut out both cards (page 47 and 49) on the dotted lines. Fold the inside of the house card (page 49) in half where shown.

4. On the front of the house, use a craft knife to carefully cut open the shutters and the door on the dotted lines. Be sure to have an adult help you with this part.

5. Put glue on inside of the house card where shown and glue the front of house to the inside of house.

6. Fold back the shutters and the door.

7. Now you can write a special Christmas message in the card. Don't forget to sign your name on the back!

Cinnamon "Cookie" Cutouts

One of my favorite Christmas traditions is trimming the tree. My family even has a tree-

trimming party every year where we eat pizza, play our favorite Christmas CDs, and tell lots and lots of stories. It's also fun to see the ornaments we've made through the years. My favorite ornaments are these cinnamon "cookie" cutouts that we made at Maria's house. It's a good thing we had plenty of cinnamon rolls and Mexican hot chocolate on hand so we weren't tempted to eat our decorations. These are the best-smelling ornaments in town!

You will need:
- *large can of cinnamon (at least 3 ounces)*
- *applesauce*
- *waxed paper*
- *cookie cutters in holiday shapes*
- *rolling pin*
- *plastic drinking straw*
- *emery board*
- *puff paint*
- *ribbon for hangers*

1. Pour almost the entire can of cinnamon into the bowl. Add

several table-spoons of applesauce and mix. Keep adding applesauce a tablespoon at a time to make a thick dough.

2. Shape the dough into a ball. Lightly dust a piece of waxed paper and the rolling pin with the rest of the cinnamon. Place the dough ball in the middle of the paper, flatten it a little with your hand, and then roll it 1/2" thick.

3. Use cookie cutters to cut out the ornaments. Dust the spatula with cin-namon and use it to lift the ornaments onto a clean piece of waxed paper.

4. Use the drinking straw to make a hole for hanging the ornaments.

5. Let the ornaments dry, turning them often—it may take several days. When they are completely dry, use the emery board to smooth any rough edges and decorate with puff paint. Hang with ribbons.

"You're an Angel" Ornaments

My favorite part of the holiday season is giving gifts to the people who mean so much to me. One year I made my favorite friends angel ornaments that told why I thought each friend was special. On Christine's I wrote, "You're an angel because you always listen to me." Aleesha's said:

"You're an angel because you're honest and truthful and funny." It was so fun to give my friends a big "thank you" gift! You can make these for your friends or for the people in your family.

You will need:
- *light posterboard*
- *tracing paper*
- *Christmas wrapping paper*
- *snapshot of person the ornament is for*
- *glue*
- *pen or marker*
- *gold or silver Christmas ribbon*

1. Trace the outline of the angel on page 56 onto tracing paper. Glue pretty and bright-colored Christmas wrapping paper to one side of a 6 1/2" by 5 1/2" piece of posterboard. Trace the angel outline onto the piece and cut out.

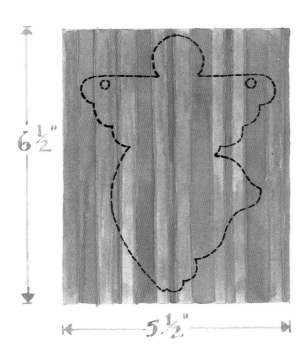

6 ½"

5 ½"

3. Cut out a picture of your friend's face and glue it in the center of the angel. Use a hole punch to put holes in the wings (see pattern) and tie a pretty ribbon to make a hanger for the tree. On the back of the ornament, write the words "You're an angel because…" Then write in some words that describe the person you're making the ornament for.

Photo

2. On a white or gold-colored doily, trace and cut out the angel. Glue the doily onto the wrapping paper side of the posterboard (the wrapping paper will show through the doily).

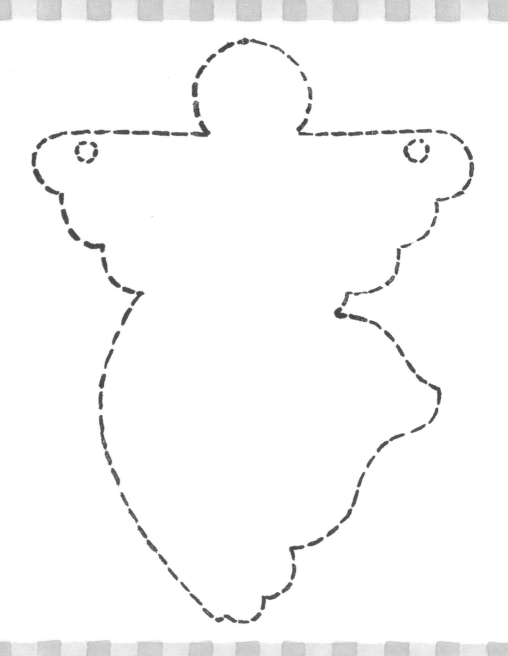

New Year's Kazoos

Elizabeth's family always has a *big* New Year's Eve party. We start early in the evening with a buffet dinner. Then we get out the games. Later Elizabeth's parents bring out fruit and dessert and some other munchies, and the games just continue! About an hour or so before midnight,

we all get going on these kazoos. They're easy to make, so we have lots of time to practice blowing them before the clock strikes twelve and everyone rings in the New Year.

You will need:
- *toilet paper tube*
- *waxed paper*
- *rubber band*
- *colored tissue paper*
- *metallic star stickers*

1. Fold the waxed paper over one end of the tube and hold it in place with the rubber band. Poke a small pinhole in the center of the waxed paper.

2. Cut a piece of tissue paper as wide as the tube and about 12" long. Cover the tube with tissue paper by wrapping the tissue several times around the roll and gluing or taping the end down.

3. Decorate the kazoo with star stickers and hum into the open end. The kazoo should make a funny buzzing noise to celebrate the New Year.

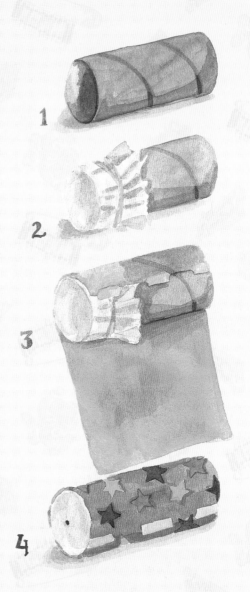

6 Let's Get Organized!

It seems like the more crafts you make, the more stuff you collect. Suddenly you have craft supplies everywhere—but you can't find anything you need for the one project you're working on! The Angels spent one afternoon making these neat boxes that keep all of our craft materials organized in one place. If you have lots of supplies, you might even want to make two of these boxes. You can also make smaller boxes for different kinds of supplies—one box for your pens, one box for stickers, one box for yarn and ribbon. We spent one Craft Day just making boxes to organize our stuff!

"Got You Covered" Boxes

Here's how you can cover any rectangular box, with or without a lid, with either paper or fabric.

You will need:

- box in any size, with or without lid
- pretty material to cover the box—fabric, wallpaper, wrapping paper, brown paper (good for stamp art!), or contact paper

- *glue stick or tacky craft glue*
- *scissors*
- *index cards and markers*

1. Lay the bottom of the box on the wrong side of the fabric or paper. To know how much fabric or paper to use, think of wrapping a present—only without a top. Instead of the paper or fabric wrapping all around the box, it falls into and over the box's top edges (see diagram 1). Cut the fabric or paper to fit your box.

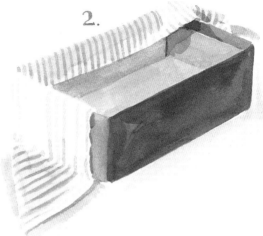

2. Using a glue stick, put glue on the outside of the box and inside the top edges where the fabric or paper will be.

3. "Wrap" fabric or paper around the box, starting on one side. When the fabric or paper covers the end of the box, it naturally folds into a triangle (diagrams 2 and 2a). Glue down all areas where the fabric or paper is touching the box.

4. Repeat the process for the other side (diagram 3).

5. On the ends, glue the fabric or paper to itself in the triangle (diagram 4).

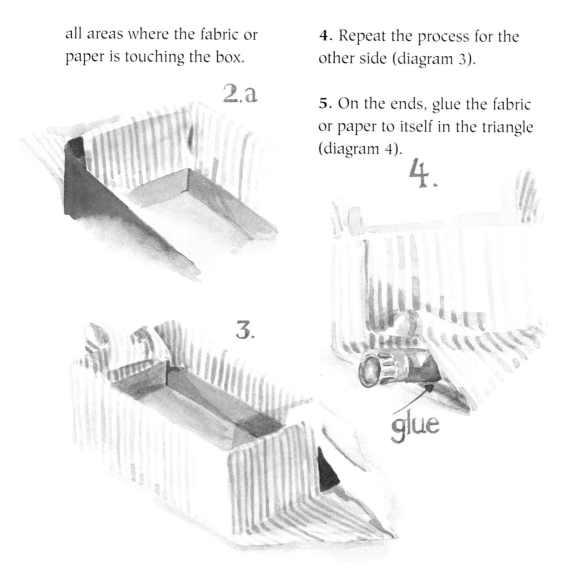

2.a

3.

4.

glue

5.

glue

6. Put glue on the top of the triangle (diagram 5) and press it up to the end of the box (diagram 6).

7. Do the lid of the box the exact same way. Just think of it as a very shallow box!

8. Decorate the box any way you like. You can add paper cutouts, stickers, buttons, or silk flowers to the box. Use index cards and markers to make labels so you'll always know what's inside your box.

6.

Whatever your hand finds to do, do it with all your might.

The Book of Ecclesiastes